# THE BUSINESS SUCCESS GUIDE TO DAIRY FARMING

Comprehensive Insight To Modern Practices, Effective Nutrition, Milking Techniques, Farm Management, And Profit Maximization

## RICHMOND HAMILL

© 2024 [RICHMOND HAMILL]. All rights reserved.

Except for brief quotations included in critical reviews and certain other noncommercial uses allowed by copyright law, no part of this book may be reproduced, distributed, or transmitted in any form or by any means, including photocopying, recording, or other electronic or mechanical methods, without the publisher's prior written permission.

# Disclaimer

The information presented in this book is based on the author's personal knowledge and understanding of livestock management. The author is not affiliated with any association, company, business, or individual in the livestock industry. All content is provided for informational purposes only and should not be considered as professional advice. Readers are encouraged to seek professional guidance and conduct their own research before making any decisions based on the information contained in this book. The author and publisher disclaim any liability for any adverse effects or consequences resulting from the use of the information contained herein.

# Table of Contents

**CHAPTER ONE** ................................................................17

Introduction To Dairy Farming .......................17

Overview Of Dairy Farming ............................17

History And Evolution Of Dairy Farming........19

Importance Of Dairy Farming In Agriculture.20

Types Of Dairy Farms........................................22

    Family Farms: ...................................................22

    Commercial Farms: ..........................................22

    Specialized Dairy Farms:.................................23

Key Benefits And Challenges Of Dairy Farming ...............................................................................24

**CHAPTER TWO** ..............................................................27

Getting Started With Dairy Farming ...............27

Selecting The Right Dairy Breed .....................27

Understanding Dairy Farm Setup Requirements ................................................... 29

Planning And Designing Your Dairy Farm ..... 30

Basic Equipment Needed For Dairy Farming .. 32

Budgeting And Financial Planning For Beginners ........................................................... 33

CHAPTER THREE ................................................. 35

Dairy Cattle Care And Management ................ 35

Daily Care Routines For Dairy Cattle .............. 35

Feeding And Nutrition Requirements ............. 37

Health Management And Common Diseases . 38

Milking Procedures And Techniques ............. 40

Record-Keeping For Cattle Health And Production ........................................................... 41

CHAPTER FOUR ................................................... 43

Milking Procedures And Techniques .............. 43

## Milking Machine Operation And Maintenance ...............43

### Milking Machine Operation .......................43

### Milking Machine Maintenance ..................44

## Manual Milking Techniques .........................46

### Preparation for Manual Milking ..................46

### Performing Manual Milking......................46

### Post-Milking Procedures ...........................47

## Hygiene And Sanitation In Milking ................48

### Importance of Hygiene in Milking..............48

### Sanitation Procedures .............................48

### Storage and Handling ..............................49

## Handling And Storage Of Milk......................50

### Handling Fresh Milk ................................50

### Storage Procedures ................................50

### Long-Term Storage .................................51

## Troubleshooting Common Milking Issues .....52

Milk Flow Problems ................................................. 52

Machine Malfunctions .............................................. 53

Hygiene Issues ........................................................... 54

## CHAPTER FIVE ........................................................ 55

Dairy Farm Infrastructure ....................................... 55

Designing And Maintaining Barns And Shelters
..................................................................................... 55

Setting Up Proper Waste Management Systems
..................................................................................... 57

Water Supply And Irrigation Systems ................. 58

Ventilation And Cooling Systems ......................... 60

Safety And Biosecurity Measures ......................... 62

## CHAPTER SIX ........................................................... 65

Feeding And Nutrition .............................................. 65

Types Of Feed And Their Nutritional Value ...... 65

Forages: ................................................................... 65

Concentrates: .......................................................... 66

Supplements: ...................................................... 66

**Formulating A Balanced Diet For Dairy Cattle** ...................................................................... 67

Assess Nutritional Requirements: ............... 67

Mixing Feeds: ............................................... 67

Feed Preparation: ........................................ 68

**Managing Pasture And Forage Crops** .............. 69

Planning and Planting: ................................ 69

Maintaining Forage Crops: ......................... 69

Harvesting and Storage: .............................. 70

**Supplementary Feeding And Additives** .......... 70

Types of Supplements: ................................ 71

Additives: ..................................................... 71

Application: ................................................. 71

**Monitoring And Adjusting Feed Plans** ............ 72

Monitoring Intake and Performance: .......... 72

Adjusting Rations: ....................................... 72

Record-Keeping and Analysis: ...... 73

## CHAPTER SEVEN ...... 75

Health And Veterinary Care ...... 75

Routine Health Checks And Vaccinations ...... 75

Identifying And Treating Common Cattle Diseases ...... 77

Preventive Care And Biosecurity Practices ...... 78

Emergency Health Management ...... 80

Working With A Veterinarian And Livestock Specialists ...... 81

## CHAPTER EIGHT ...... 83

Reproduction And Breeding ...... 83

Understanding Dairy Cattle Reproduction Cycles ...... 83

Breeding Methods And Selecting Breeding Stock ...... 84

Managing Pregnancies And Calving ...... 86

Caring For Newborn Calves ............................ 87

Record-Keeping For Breeding And
Reproduction ................................................... 89

## CHAPTER NINE ................................................ 91

Dairy Farm Operations And Management ...... 91

Daily Farm Management Tasks ....................... 91

Financial Management And Record-Keeping . 93

Labor Management And Training ................... 94

Marketing And Selling Dairy Products ........... 96

Implementing Sustainable Farming Practices
........................................................................... 97

## CHAPTER TEN .................................................. 101

Troubleshooting Common Issues ................... 101

Identifying And Solving Common Dairy
Farming Problems ........................................... 101

Addressing Equipment Failures And Repairs 102

**Handling Unexpected Health And Production Issues** .................................................................. 104

**Dealing With Market Fluctuations** ................. 106

**Seeking Support And Resources For Problem-Solving** ............................................................ 107

**Frequently Asked A Question And Their Answers** ............................................................. 111

**CONCLUSION** .................................................. 118

**THE END** ......................................................... 122

## ABOUT THIS BOOK

"Dairy Farming" is an essential guide for both aspiring and established dairy farmers, offering a comprehensive exploration of the industry. This book delves into every facet of dairy farming, starting with a detailed overview of its history and evolution, underscoring its significance in agriculture. It introduces various types of dairy farms, from family-operated to large commercial enterprises, highlighting the key benefits and challenges associated with each.

For those venturing into dairy farming, this book provides crucial insights on selecting the right dairy breed and setting up a farm. It covers the necessary planning and design considerations, and basic equipment requirements, and offers guidance on budgeting and financial planning to ensure a successful start.

The heart of dairy farming lies in effective cattle care and management. This book guides readers through daily care routines, feeding and nutrition requirements, health management, and milking procedures. Emphasis is placed on maintaining detailed records to monitor cattle health and production, ensuring the highest standards of care and efficiency.

Milking procedures and techniques are addressed with a focus on both manual and machine methods. This book provides practical advice on operating and maintaining milking machines, ensuring hygiene and sanitation, and troubleshooting common milking issues.

Infrastructure plays a pivotal role in dairy farming, and this book offers in-depth guidance on designing and maintaining barns and shelters, setting up waste management systems, and ensuring proper water supply, ventilation, and biosecurity measures.

Feeding and nutrition are further explored, with sections dedicated to understanding different types of feed, formulating balanced diets, managing pastures, and using supplements effectively.

Health and veterinary care are integral to successful dairy farming. This book covers routine health checks, disease management, preventive care, and emergency health management, alongside advice on working with veterinarians and livestock specialists.

Reproduction and breeding are crucial for maintaining a productive herd. This book explains dairy cattle reproduction cycles, breeding methods, pregnancy management, and newborn calf care, stressing the importance of detailed record-keeping.

Operational aspects of dairy farming, including daily management tasks, financial oversight, labor management, and marketing, are thoroughly covered.

This book also addresses sustainable farming practices, ensuring that readers can implement environmentally friendly and economically viable strategies.

Finally, this book provides practical solutions for troubleshooting common issues, from equipment failures to market fluctuations. It offers guidance on seeking support and resources, equipping dairy farmers with the tools needed to navigate and resolve challenges effectively.

Overall, "Dairy Farming" stands as an invaluable resource for anyone involved in or considering entering the dairy industry, providing expert knowledge and practical advice to help achieve success in this vital sector.

# CHAPTER ONE

## Introduction To Dairy Farming

## Overview Of Dairy Farming

Dairy farming involves the breeding and raising of cows specifically for milk production. It is an agricultural practice where farmers manage the health, nutrition, and breeding of dairy cattle to produce milk and other dairy products. At its core, dairy farming focuses on ensuring the cows' well-being to maximize milk yield and quality. This practice can vary significantly in scale, from small family-run operations to large commercial enterprises.

In a typical dairy farm, the primary goal is to maintain a high level of milk production while ensuring the health and comfort of the cows.

This involves providing a suitable environment, proper nutrition, regular veterinary care, and efficient milking processes. The operation often includes facilities like milking parlors, feed storage areas, and housing for the cattle. Modern dairy farming also integrates advanced technology, such as automated milking systems and herd management software, to enhance productivity and efficiency.

For beginners, starting a dairy farm involves understanding the basics of dairy cattle management, including breed selection, feeding practices, and milking techniques. Farmers need to familiarize themselves with animal husbandry principles, as well as regulatory requirements related to animal welfare and food safety. Additionally, setting up a dairy farm requires careful planning of infrastructure and equipment, which can be achieved by seeking advice from experienced dairy farmers and agricultural extension services.

# History And Evolution Of Dairy Farming

Dairy farming has a long history that dates back thousands of years. The practice began around 10,000 years ago when early humans domesticated cattle and began milking them for their nutritional benefits. Over time, dairy farming evolved from a rudimentary practice to a sophisticated industry. Early methods were simple, involving hand milking and basic tools, but technological advancements have transformed dairy farming into a highly efficient and mechanized industry.

During the 18th and 19th centuries, dairy farming saw significant improvements with the introduction of new breeds of dairy cattle, such as the Holstein and Jersey. These breeds were specifically selected for their high milk production capabilities. The development of pasteurization and refrigeration in the late 19th and early 20th centuries further revolutionized dairy farming by improving milk safety and extending its shelf life.

In the modern era, dairy farming has embraced automation and technology. Innovations such as robotic milking systems, precision feeding, and data-driven herd management have greatly enhanced productivity and animal welfare. Understanding this evolution helps new farmers appreciate the progress in dairy farming practices and adapt modern techniques to their operations.

## Importance Of Dairy Farming In Agriculture

Dairy farming plays a crucial role in agriculture and food systems worldwide. It provides a significant source of nutrition, including essential proteins, vitamins, and minerals, to people across the globe. Milk and dairy products such as cheese, yogurt, and butter are staples in many diets, making dairy farming a vital component of food security.

Economically, dairy farming contributes substantially to the agricultural sector by creating jobs and generating income for farmers and rural communities. It supports various ancillary industries, including feed production, equipment manufacturing, and dairy processing. The dairy sector also plays a role in land management and conservation, as many dairy farms use grazing practices that help maintain open landscapes and support biodiversity.

For beginners, understanding the importance of dairy farming highlights its potential impact on local and global scales. It emphasizes the need for responsible farming practices that ensure both economic viability and environmental sustainability. Engaging in dairy farming can be a rewarding endeavor that contributes positively to food systems and community well-being.

## Types Of Dairy Farms

Dairy farms can vary widely in size and scope, generally categorized into several types based on their scale and production methods.

**Family Farms:** These are typically smaller operations where the family manages all aspects of the dairy farm, from milking to feeding and herd management. Family farms often focus on producing high-quality milk and maintaining traditional farming practices. These farms may have a limited number of cows and rely on manual milking or smaller-scale equipment.

**Commercial Farms:** Commercial dairy farms are larger operations that focus on maximizing production and efficiency.

They often employ advanced technologies, such as automated milking systems, precision feeding, and large-scale processing facilities. These farms may produce milk on a large scale for distribution to major retailers and processors.

**Specialized Dairy Farms:** Some dairy farms specialize in niche markets, such as organic dairy farming or producing specialty dairy products like cheese or yogurt. These farms may adhere to specific production methods or certification standards that appeal to particular consumer segments.

For beginners, choosing the type of dairy farm to start depends on factors such as available resources, market opportunities, and personal preferences. Each type has its own set of requirements and challenges, so it is essential to thoroughly research and plan according to the chosen model.

# Key Benefits And Challenges Of Dairy Farming

Dairy farming offers numerous benefits, including the production of nutritious food products, job creation, and economic contribution to rural areas. It supports local economies by providing employment opportunities in farming, processing, and distribution. Additionally, dairy farming can promote environmental stewardship through practices like rotational grazing and manure recycling, which can enhance soil health and reduce waste.

However, dairy farming also presents challenges that need to be addressed. These include managing the health and welfare of dairy cattle, dealing with fluctuating milk prices, and adhering to environmental regulations.

Farmers must also contend with issues related to feed costs, disease management, and labor shortages.

To overcome these challenges, beginners should invest in knowledge and training, seek advice from experienced dairy farmers, and stay informed about industry best practices. Implementing effective herd management strategies, maintaining high standards of animal welfare, and adopting innovative technologies can help mitigate these challenges and ensure a successful dairy farming operation.

# CHAPTER TWO

## Getting Started With Dairy Farming

## Selecting The Right Dairy Breed

Choosing the right dairy breed is crucial for a successful dairy farming venture. The breed you select will impact milk production, herd management, and overall profitability. Begin by evaluating the primary dairy breeds: Holstein, Jersey, Guernsey, and Ayrshire, among others. Holsteins are renowned for their high milk yield and are the most common breed in commercial dairy operations. They are large, with distinctive black-and-white markings, and are known for their adaptability to various climates.

Jerseys, on the other hand, are smaller in size and produce milk with higher butterfat content. They are ideal for farms focusing on cheese or butter production. Guernseys are valued for their rich, golden milk, which is also high in butterfat and protein, making them a good choice for specialized dairy products. Ayrshires are hardy and thrive in various conditions, offering a good balance between milk quantity and quality.

To select the right breed, consider your farm's goals, the climate of your location, and the specific milk quality or quantity you aim to achieve. Consult with local dairy farmers or agricultural extension services for advice tailored to your region. Additionally, visiting farms that use the breeds you are interested in can provide practical insights and help you make an informed decision.

# Understanding Dairy Farm Setup Requirements

Setting up a dairy farm involves several key considerations to ensure a smooth operation. Start by assessing the land area you have available. Dairy cows require ample space, both for grazing and for housing. Each cow needs around 100 square feet of space in the barn and 2 to 3 acres of pasture per cow for grazing. Additionally, ensure that the land has good drainage to prevent waterlogging, which can lead to health issues for the cows.

Next, consider the infrastructure needed. You'll need a milking parlor equipped with milking machines, a dairy barn for housing the cows, and storage facilities for feed and bedding materials. Ensure that the barn is well-ventilated and has proper waste management systems in place to handle manure and other byproducts efficiently.

An access road or pathway for the transportation of feed and equipment is also essential.

Water supply is another critical factor. Cows drink a significant amount of water daily, so ensure a reliable source of clean, fresh water. Install water troughs or automatic waterers to ensure constant access. Additionally, plan for waste management by setting up a manure storage area and a composting system or manure spreader to manage waste sustainably.

## Planning And Designing Your Dairy Farm

Effective planning and design are fundamental to setting up a successful dairy farm. Start by creating a detailed farm layout that includes all essential areas such as barns, milking parlors, feed storage, and waste management systems. Use a scale drawing to map out the location of each component, ensuring there is enough space for future expansion.

In designing your dairy barn, consider the flow of operations. The barn should be designed to facilitate easy movement of cows from the feeding area to the milking parlor and back. This minimizes stress for the animals and improves efficiency. Include separate areas for feeding, resting, and milking, with easy access for cleaning and maintenance.

Invest in designing a well-organized feed storage area. Proper feed storage ensures that your feed remains fresh and free from contamination. Consider incorporating silos or bulk bins and ensure they are easily accessible from both the feeding area and delivery trucks. Additionally, plan for proper ventilation to keep feed dry and prevent mold growth.

# Basic Equipment Needed For Dairy Farming

Starting a dairy farm requires several pieces of essential equipment to ensure smooth operations. Begin with milking equipment, including milking machines, which automate the milking process and increase efficiency. Milking machines consist of a vacuum pump, milking units, and a pipeline system that transfers milk to the bulk tank.

Invest in a bulk tank to store the milk. Bulk tanks are designed to keep milk at the proper temperature and prevent spoilage. Ensure that the tank is sized according to your herd size and milk production levels. Additionally, you'll need a feed mixer to blend various feed components and ensure a balanced diet for your cows.

Other essential equipment includes a manure spreader for waste management, a tractor for farm operations, and a water heater for maintaining optimal water temperatures. Regular maintenance of this equipment is crucial to prevent breakdowns and ensure long-term efficiency.

## Budgeting And Financial Planning For Beginners

Budgeting and financial planning are vital for the success of your dairy farm. Start by estimating the initial capital required for land acquisition, infrastructure development, and equipment purchase. Consider additional costs for livestock, feed, veterinary care, and ongoing operational expenses. Creating a detailed business plan will help you outline these costs and set financial goals.

Monitor your cash flow closely to manage expenses effectively. Track all income and expenditures to ensure you stay within budget. It's advisable to set aside a contingency fund for unexpected costs such as equipment repairs or veterinary emergencies. Explore financing options such as loans or grants specifically designed for agricultural ventures.

Consider working with a financial advisor who specializes in agriculture to help you develop a sound financial strategy. They can assist with budgeting, tax planning, and investment decisions to ensure your dairy farm remains financially viable and profitable in the long run. Regularly review and adjust your financial plan based on actual performance and market conditions.

# CHAPTER THREE

## Dairy Cattle Care And Management

## Daily Care Routines For Dairy Cattle

Ensuring proper daily care routines for dairy cattle is essential for their health and productivity. Daily care includes tasks such as feeding, watering, grooming, and monitoring overall health. Start the day by checking each animal individually. Inspect their general condition, especially their coat, eyes, and demeanor, as these can indicate health issues. Ensure they have access to clean water at all times, as dairy cows require plenty of water to stay hydrated, especially during lactation.

Feeding dairy cattle involves providing a balanced diet rich in nutrients like protein, carbohydrates, vitamins, and minerals. Hay, silage, and grains are common components, tailored to meet the specific nutritional needs of lactating cows. It's crucial to maintain a consistent feeding schedule and adjust rations based on the cow's stage of lactation and body condition score. Monitor feed intake to ensure each cow is consuming enough to support milk production without excessive weight gain.

Grooming is another vital aspect of daily care. Regularly brush the cows to remove dirt and debris, which helps prevent skin issues and keeps them comfortable. Pay attention to hoof health as well, trimming them regularly to prevent lameness and other foot problems. Lastly, ensure that the barn or shelter is clean and well-ventilated, providing a comfortable environment conducive to dairy cow health and productivity.

# Feeding And Nutrition Requirements

Feeding dairy cattle requires a nuanced approach to meet their specific nutritional requirements. The diet must support milk production, reproductive health, and overall well-being. Typically, dairy cows consume a combination of roughage (hay or pasture) and concentrates (grains and protein supplements). The ratio and type of feed vary depending on factors such as lactation stage, body condition, and the quality of available forage.

During early lactation, cows have high energy demands, necessitating diets rich in carbohydrates and proteins. As lactation progresses, adjustments are made to maintain milk yield while managing the cow's body condition score. Fiber is crucial for rumen health, aiding digestion and preventing metabolic issues like acidosis.

Mineral supplements, such as calcium and phosphorus, are essential for bone strength and milk quality.

Monitoring feed intake and cow behavior helps assess nutritional adequacy and adjust diets accordingly. Providing clean water is equally vital, as dairy cows consume large quantities, especially during hot weather or high milk production periods. Consulting with a nutritionist or veterinarian can help formulate diets tailored to individual cow needs, optimizing health and milk production.

## Health Management And Common Diseases

Maintaining dairy cattle health requires proactive management strategies to prevent diseases and treat illnesses promptly. Regular veterinary inspections and vaccinations are essential components of health management.

Vaccines protect against common diseases such as mastitis, respiratory infections, and reproductive disorders. Implementing a biosecurity plan helps minimize the risk of introducing pathogens to the herd.

Monitoring cow health involves daily observations and periodic health checks. Look for signs of illness, such as decreased appetite, lethargy, changes in milk production, or abnormal behaviors. Promptly isolate sick cows to prevent disease spread and provide appropriate treatment under veterinary guidance. Good hygiene practices, including clean bedding and udder care during milking, reduce the risk of infections.

Implementing a herd health program includes regular deworming, parasite control, and maintaining optimal body condition through balanced nutrition and exercise. Keeping accurate health records aids in tracking vaccinations, treatments, and reproductive cycles, facilitating timely interventions and herd health assessments.

## Milking Procedures And Techniques

Efficient milking procedures are critical for dairy cow welfare and milk quality. Start by preparing the milking area, ensuring the cleanliness and functionality of the milking equipment. Wash udders and teats with a sanitizing solution before milking to prevent bacterial contamination. Proper teat stimulation and pre-milking routines help initiate milk let-downs and ensure complete udder emptying.

During milking, observe each cow for signs of mastitis or other udder abnormalities. Use appropriate milking techniques to minimize stress and discomfort for the cows while maximizing milk yield. Post-milking teat disinfection reduces the risk of infections and maintains udder health. Properly store and handle milk to preserve quality and safety standards, adhering to regulatory guidelines for milk production.

## Record-Keeping For Cattle Health And Production

Effective record-keeping is essential for managing dairy cattle health and optimizing production efficiency. Maintain comprehensive records documenting each cow's health history, including vaccinations, treatments, and reproductive cycles. Track milk production data, such as yield per cow and milk quality parameters, to monitor productivity trends and identify potential issues early.

Recording feed intake and nutritional adjustments helps evaluate diet effectiveness and tailor feeding programs to individual cow needs. Keep detailed records of breeding dates, pregnancies, and calving outcomes to manage reproductive cycles and plant breeding strategies. Analyzing historical data facilitates informed decision-making regarding herd management practices, health interventions, and financial planning.

Utilize digital tools or management software to streamline record-keeping processes and ensure data accuracy. Regularly review and analyze records to identify patterns, trends, or deviations that may require attention or adjustment. Collaborate with veterinarians and nutritionists to interpret data and implement targeted interventions, optimizing dairy cattle health, welfare, and production outcomes.

# CHAPTER FOUR

## Milking Procedures And Techniques

## Milking Machine Operation And Maintenance

### Milking Machine Operation

Operating a milking machine involves a series of straightforward steps to ensure efficient and hygienic milking. Begin by preparing the milking machine for use. Ensure that all components, including the milking units, vacuum pump, and milk collection system, are clean and in good working condition. Before attaching the machine to the cows, turn on the vacuum pump to create the necessary vacuum pressure. This vacuum pressure helps in the extraction of milk from the udder.

Adjust the vacuum pressure according to the manufacturer's guidelines, typically between 38-42 kPa (kilopascals) for optimal milking.

Attach the milking units to the cow's teats, ensuring that the liners are correctly aligned and that the units are properly secured. The machine should be adjusted so that it fits comfortably around the teats without causing any discomfort to the cow. Once attached, the milking machine will begin the milking process. Monitor the machine closely to ensure that it operates smoothly, and listen for any unusual noises that may indicate a problem. Regularly check the milk flow rate and the vacuum pressure during milking to maintain efficiency.

Milking Machine Maintenance

Proper maintenance of the milking machine is crucial for its longevity and performance. After each milking session, disassemble the machine and thoroughly clean all components, including the liners, tea cups, and milk collection bucket. Use a sanitizing solution recommended by the manufacturer to ensure that all milk residues and bacteria are removed. Rinse all parts with clean water and allow them to air dry completely before reassembly.

Regularly inspect the machine for signs of wear and tear. Check the vacuum pump, pipelines, and connections for any leaks or damage. Replace any worn-out or damaged parts promptly to avoid disruptions in milking. Schedule periodic professional maintenance to ensure that the machine is operating at peak performance. Follow the manufacturer's maintenance schedule and guidelines to prevent any long-term issues and ensure the machine's efficiency and reliability.

# Manual Milking Techniques

## Preparation for Manual Milking

Manual milking requires a hands-on approach and a good understanding of cow anatomy and milking techniques. Before starting, ensure that you have all the necessary equipment, including a clean bucket for collecting milk and a gentle udder cleanser. Begin by preparing the cow for milking. Lead the cow to a clean and comfortable milking area. Wash your hands thoroughly and clean the cow's udder with warm water and a mild disinfectant to remove any dirt and bacteria. Dry the udder with a clean towel to avoid contaminating the milk.

## Performing Manual Milking

To start milking, position yourself comfortably next to the cow. Gently grasp one of the teats with your thumb and forefinger, and apply steady, gentle pressure. Begin by squeezing and pulling downwards in a rhythmic motion, using your other fingers to support and guide the milk flow. It's essential to apply even pressure to prevent discomfort for the cow and to maximize milk extraction. Continue this process, alternating between teats to maintain a consistent milk flow and avoid overworking one teat.

## Post-Milking Procedures

After milking, clean the udder again to prevent any infections and maintain hygiene. Transfer the milk to a clean, sanitized container. Store the milk immediately in a cool, clean environment to preserve its quality. Thoroughly clean the milking equipment and area to ensure that no residual milk or bacteria remain, which could affect future milk quality or cause hygiene issues.

# Hygiene And Sanitation In Milking

## Importance of Hygiene in Milking

Maintaining high standards of hygiene during milking is crucial for producing quality milk and preventing contamination. Start by ensuring that the milking area, equipment, and the cows themselves are clean. The milking parlor or barn should be regularly cleaned and disinfected to prevent the build-up of bacteria. Milkers should always wash their hands thoroughly before handling any equipment or coming into contact with the cows.

## Sanitation Procedures

Before milking, clean the udder of the cow with a disinfectant solution to remove any dirt or bacteria. Use separate, disposable, or easily sanitized towels for each cow to avoid cross-contamination. After milking, clean and sanitize all milking equipment, including the milking machine, buckets, and any other tools used during the process. Use hot water and appropriate cleaning agents to remove any milk residues. Rinse all equipment thoroughly to ensure that no cleaning agents remain that could affect the milk quality.

## Storage and Handling

Proper storage of milk is essential to maintaining its freshness and safety. After milking, transfer the milk to clean, sanitized containers and refrigerate immediately. Maintain the refrigeration temperature between 4-7°C (39-45°F) to inhibit bacterial growth. Ensure that the milk storage area is also clean and well-maintained. Regularly check for any signs of spoilage or contamination, and follow proper protocols for handling and disposing of any spoiled milk.

# Handling And Storage Of Milk

## Handling Fresh Milk

Handling milk with care is essential to preserving its quality. After milking, immediately transfer the milk to clean, sanitized containers. Use containers made of food-grade materials to prevent any contamination. Handle the milk gently to avoid agitation, which can lead to the breakdown of milk proteins and affect the milk's texture and flavor. Ensure that all milk-handling practices adhere to hygiene standards to prevent contamination and spoilage.

## Storage Procedures

Milk should be stored in a cool, clean environment to maintain its freshness. Refrigerate the milk as soon as possible, ideally within 30 minutes of milking, at a temperature between 4-7°C (39-45°F).

This temperature range helps inhibit bacterial growth and extends the milk's shelf life. Store milk in airtight containers to prevent absorption of odors and flavors from other substances. Regularly check and clean the storage equipment, such as refrigerators or coolers, to ensure that they are functioning properly and maintaining the correct temperature.

Long-Term Storage

For long-term storage, consider pasteurizing the milk to kill any harmful bacteria. Pasteurization involves heating the milk to a specific temperature for a set period and then cooling it quickly. This process can help extend the milk's shelf life and improve its safety. If storing milk for extended periods, use proper packaging methods and label containers with the date of milking to ensure proper rotation and use. Regularly inspect stored milk for any signs of spoilage, such as off smells or changes in texture, and discard any milk that does not meet quality standards.

## Troubleshooting Common Milking Issues

### Milk Flow Problems

One common issue during milking is inadequate milk flow, which can be caused by various factors, including improper milking machine settings, udder health issues, or incorrect milking techniques. Check the milking machine's vacuum pressure and ensure it is set according to the manufacturer's specifications. Inspect the cow's udder for any signs of infection or damage that could affect milk flow. Adjust your milking technique to ensure even pressure and rhythmic milking.

If the problem persists, consult a veterinarian or a milking equipment specialist for further assistance.

## Machine Malfunctions

Milking machine malfunctions can disrupt the milking process and affect milk quality. Common issues include leaks in the vacuum system, malfunctioning pulsators, or worn-out liners. Regularly inspect the machine for any visible signs of damage or wear. If you encounter a problem, first check for leaks or blockages in the vacuum system and ensure all connections are secure. Test the pulsators to ensure they are functioning correctly and replace any damaged or worn parts. For more complex issues, refer to the machine's manual or seek professional repair services.

## Hygiene Issues

Poor hygiene can lead to contamination and spoilage of milk. If you notice any unusual odors or off-flavors in the milk, it may indicate a hygiene problem. Review your cleaning and sanitizing procedures to ensure they are thorough and effective. Check that all milking equipment is properly cleaned and that the milking environment is maintained to prevent contamination. Regularly monitor milk quality and adhere to strict hygiene practices to prevent recurring issues. If necessary, seek advice from a dairy hygiene expert to address persistent problems and improve your milking practices.

# CHAPTER FIVE

## Dairy Farm Infrastructure

## Designing And Maintaining Barns And Shelters

Designing and maintaining barns and shelters is a crucial aspect of dairy farming that directly impacts the health and productivity of your herd. Proper barn design should prioritize space, ventilation, and comfort to ensure the well-being of your cows. Begin by determining the number of cows you plan to house, as this will dictate the size and layout of your barn. Each cow typically requires around 100 to 120 square feet of space, depending on the breed and housing system you choose.

For effective barn design, consider using a free-stall barn layout, where cows have individual stalls to rest in while roaming freely in the barn.

This type of system helps reduce stress and allows for natural behaviors, promoting overall health. Ensure the barn is well-ventilated, with proper airflow to remove excess moisture and heat. This can be achieved by incorporating ridge vents, sidewall openings, and ceiling fans. Proper lighting is also essential, with natural light being preferable for both the cows and the workers. Artificial lighting should mimic natural daylight to help regulate the cows' circadian rhythms.

Maintaining the barn involves regular cleaning and inspections. Manure should be removed frequently to prevent the buildup of pathogens and odors. Floors should be non-slip and easy to clean, ideally made of concrete with a rough surface. Regularly inspect and repair any damaged structures to ensure safety and comfort. Implementing a routine cleaning schedule for feed bins, water troughs, and stalls is essential for maintaining hygiene and preventing disease outbreaks.

## Setting Up Proper Waste Management Systems

An efficient waste management system is vital for maintaining a clean and healthy dairy farm. Manure management involves collecting, storing, and disposing of manure in a way that minimizes environmental impact and optimizes its use as a resource. Start by selecting an appropriate manure collection system based on your barn design. Common options include gutter systems or slatted floors that direct manure to a central collection area.

Manure should be collected regularly to prevent accumulation and reduce odor. For storage, use manure pits or lagoons, ensuring they are properly lined to prevent contamination of groundwater. The size and design of your storage facility should account for the volume of manure produced and the length of time it will be stored. Proper management of the storage area involves regular inspections and maintenance to prevent leaks and odors.

Manure can be used as a valuable fertilizer for crops, reducing the need for synthetic fertilizers. To utilize manure effectively, consider setting up a composting system. This involves mixing manure with bedding material to create compost, which can then be applied to fields. Ensure that composting is done in a designated area away from water sources to prevent runoff. Regular turning of the compost pile is necessary to maintain aerobic conditions and accelerate decomposition.

## Water Supply And Irrigation Systems

Providing a reliable water supply is essential for dairy cattle health and milk production. Begin by assessing your farm's water needs based on the number of cows and the local climate. Each cow requires approximately 30 to 50 gallons of water per day, so ensure your water source can meet this demand. Options include wells, surface water sources, or municipal supplies, with wells being a common choice for many dairy farms due to their reliability.

Install a water distribution system that includes pipes, troughs, and automatic waterers to ensure easy access for your cows. Automatic waterers help maintain a constant water supply and minimize waste. Ensure that waterers are placed at an appropriate height for easy access and are regularly cleaned to prevent contamination. Insulate water pipes in colder climates to prevent freezing and ensure a consistent water supply year-round.

In addition to providing water for drinking, consider implementing an irrigation system for crops. Proper irrigation helps maintain healthy forage and feed crops, which are crucial for dairy cow nutrition.

Common irrigation methods include sprinkler systems, drip irrigation, and flood irrigation. Choose a system that suits your farm's layout and crop types. Regular maintenance and monitoring of irrigation systems are essential to ensure efficient water use and avoid over- or under-watering.

## Ventilation And Cooling Systems

Effective ventilation and cooling systems are critical for maintaining a comfortable environment for dairy cattle. Cows are sensitive to heat stress, which can negatively impact their milk production and overall health. Begin by assessing your barn's ventilation needs based on its size, design, and the local climate. Proper ventilation helps remove excess heat, moisture, and odors while bringing in fresh air.

Incorporate natural ventilation by designing your barn with adequate openings, such as ridge vents and sidewall curtains, to facilitate airflow.

Ceiling fans and exhaust fans can be used to enhance air movement and improve cooling. During hot weather, consider installing misting or evaporative cooling systems to reduce the temperature in the barn. These systems use water to create a fine mist that evaporates, cooling the air and providing relief to the cows.

Regular maintenance of ventilation and cooling systems is essential to ensure their effectiveness. Clean fans, filters, and cooling pads regularly to prevent dust and debris buildup. Inspect and repair any damaged components promptly. Monitoring the barn's temperature and humidity levels using sensors or thermometers helps ensure that the cooling systems are operating efficiently and maintaining a comfortable environment for your cows.

# Safety And Biosecurity Measures

Implementing safety and biosecurity measures is crucial for protecting your dairy herd from diseases and ensuring a safe working environment. Begin by establishing a biosecurity plan that includes protocols for managing visitors, handling animals, and preventing disease transmission. Limit access to the farm to authorized personnel and provide visitors with protective clothing, such as coveralls and boots.

Regularly disinfect equipment, tools, and facilities to reduce the risk of spreading pathogens. Use approved disinfectants and follow the manufacturer's instructions for proper application. Establish a routine for cleaning and sanitizing feed and water troughs, stalls, and bedding materials. Implement a quarantine protocol for new or sick animals to prevent the introduction of diseases to the rest of the herd.

In addition to biosecurity measures, ensure that your farm's infrastructure is safe and well-maintained. This includes inspecting fences, gates, and barn structures for damage and repairing them as needed. Provide adequate lighting in all areas to reduce the risk of accidents. Implement safety training for all farm workers to ensure they are aware of proper procedures for handling animals, operating machinery, and responding to emergencies.

# CHAPTER SIX

## Feeding And Nutrition

## Types Of Feed And Their Nutritional Value

In dairy farming, understanding the types of feed and their nutritional value is crucial for ensuring the health and productivity of your dairy cattle. The primary categories of feed are forages, concentrates, and supplements.

Forages: Forages include grasses, legumes, and silages. Alfalfa hay and clover are rich in protein and fiber, making them essential for digestion and overall health. Silage, made from fermented green foliage, provides high energy and helps maintain gut health. Understanding the maturity of these plants is key; younger, leafy forages are more nutritious compared to older, stemmy ones.

Concentrates: These are energy-dense feeds such as grains (corn, barley, oats) and protein sources (soybean meal, canola meal). Concentrates are essential for increasing the energy and protein levels in the diet, especially when milk production is high. Grains should be processed (ground, cracked, or rolled) to improve digestibility. However, over-reliance on concentrates can lead to digestive issues and metabolic disorders.

Supplements: These include minerals, vitamins, and special additives like probiotics and prebiotics. Minerals like calcium, phosphorus, and magnesium are vital for bone health and milk production. Vitamin supplements ensure that cattle receive necessary nutrients not always present in forage or concentrate feeds.

Probiotics aid digestion and boost immune function, while prebiotics help maintain a healthy gut microbiome.

# Formulating A Balanced Diet For Dairy Cattle

Formulating a balanced diet for dairy cattle involves combining various feeds to meet their nutritional requirements for optimal milk production and overall health. The basic approach is to ensure a proper balance of energy, protein, fiber, vitamins, and minerals.

**Assess Nutritional Requirements:** Begin by assessing the nutritional needs based on the stage of lactation, body weight, and production level of the cattle. Lactating cows have higher energy and protein requirements compared to dry cows or heifers. Use nutritional guidelines and software tools to calculate the specific needs of each cow.

**Mixing Feeds:** Create a ration that combines forages, concentrates, and supplements to meet the calculated nutritional needs. For example, a typical dairy ration might include 60% forages (e.g., alfalfa hay), 30% concentrates (e.g., corn and soybean meal), and 10% supplements (e.g., mineral mix and vitamin supplements). Ensure that the fiber content is adequate to support proper digestion.

**Feed Preparation:** Use a feed mixer or a similar tool to combine the ingredients thoroughly. This step is crucial to ensure that each mouthful of feed has a consistent nutrient profile. If possible, use a TMR (Total Mixed ratio) approach where all components are mixed, reducing the risk of selective feeding and nutrient imbalances.

# Managing Pasture And Forage Crops

Effective management of pasture and forage crops is essential for providing high-quality feed and ensuring sustainability in dairy farming. This involves planning, planting, maintaining, and harvesting.

**Planning and Planting:** Choose forage crops suited to your local climate and soil type. Common choices include alfalfa, clover, and various grasses. Prepare the soil by testing for pH and nutrient levels, and amend it as needed. Planting should be done at the optimal time for each crop species, typically in the spring or early summer.

**Maintaining Forage Crops:** Regularly monitor the growth of forage crops. Implement practices such as rotational grazing to prevent overgrazing and maintain soil health. Fertilize and irrigate according to the specific needs of the crops to ensure vigorous growth and high yield.

**Harvesting and Storage:** Harvest forage crops at the right stage of maturity to maximize nutritional value. For example, hay should be cut before it reaches full maturity to ensure high protein content. Proper drying and storage in bales or silage bags prevent spoilage and preserve quality. Regularly check stored forage for mold or rot and take corrective measures if necessary.

## Supplementary Feeding And Additives

Supplementary feeding and additives are used to address specific nutritional deficiencies or to enhance the overall diet of dairy cattle. This practice helps to fine-tune the diet and improve cattle performance.

Types of Supplements: Common supplements include protein meals (soybean or canola), energy supplements (corn gluten or barley), and mineral mixes. Use supplements to correct imbalances in the main feed ingredients or to meet specific nutritional needs that are not fully addressed by forages and concentrates.

Additives: Feed additives such as yeast products, probiotics, and enzymes can improve digestion and nutrient utilization. For instance, yeast products can enhance rumen fermentation, leading to better feed efficiency. Enzymes can aid in breaking down fibrous plant material, making nutrients more available.

Application: Supplements and additives should be incorporated into the diet based on the results of regular nutritional assessments and feed tests. Follow recommended dosages and guidelines to avoid over-supplementation, which can lead to health issues or wastage. Consult with a nutritionist or veterinarian for tailored recommendations and adjustments.

## Monitoring And Adjusting Feed Plans

Ongoing monitoring and adjustment of feed plans are essential to maintain optimal health and productivity in dairy cattle. Regular assessments help in fine-tuning diets and addressing any issues that arise.

**Monitoring Intake and Performance:** Regularly observe cattle for signs of health issues, changes in milk production, and overall body condition. Record feed intake and monitor milk yield to identify any discrepancies between expected and actual performance.

**Adjusting Rations:** Based on performance data, adjust rations to correct any deficiencies or imbalances. For instance, if milk production drops, evaluate the current diet and consider increasing energy or protein levels. Regularly review feed costs and availability to make cost-effective adjustments without compromising nutritional quality.

Record-Keeping and Analysis: Maintain detailed records of feed formulations, intake levels, and cattle performance. Use this data to analyze trends and make informed decisions. Periodic reviews with a nutritionist or feed consultant can provide additional insights and recommendations for optimizing the feeding program.

By following these guidelines, dairy farmers can ensure that their cattle receive a well-balanced diet that supports health and maximizes milk production.

# CHAPTER SEVEN

## Health And Veterinary Care

## Routine Health Checks And Vaccinations

Routine health checks and vaccinations are fundamental to maintaining a healthy dairy herd. These practices help prevent the outbreak of diseases, ensure cattle are growing properly, and increase overall productivity. Begin by establishing a regular schedule for health checks. This typically includes visual inspections of each cow to monitor for signs of illness, such as changes in behavior, appetite, or physical appearance. Pay attention to vital signs like temperature, heart rate, and respiration, and make note of any deviations from normal ranges.

Vaccinations are another critical aspect of routine health care. Develop a vaccination schedule in consultation with your veterinarian, focusing on diseases common to your region and your herd's specific needs. Common vaccinations include those for bovine respiratory disease (BRD), mastitis, and foot-and-mouth disease. Ensure vaccinations are administered according to the manufacturer's guidelines and records are kept up to date. This helps track the herd's health history and ensure timely follow-ups.

In addition to vaccinations, regular deworming and parasite control are essential. Administer dewormers as recommended by your veterinarian, and monitor the herd for signs of parasite infestations. Maintaining proper sanitation in the barn and feeding areas can help minimize the risk of parasitic infections.

# Identifying And Treating Common Cattle Diseases

Identifying and treating common cattle diseases involves a keen eye and a systematic approach. Start by familiarizing yourself with the symptoms of prevalent diseases such as mastitis, lumpy skin disease, and brucellosis. Mastitis, for example, is characterized by swelling, heat, and pain in the udder, along with changes in milk quality. Early detection is crucial, and affected cows should be isolated and treated promptly.

Treatment typically involves administering antibiotics or other medications as prescribed by your veterinarian. It's important to follow dosage instructions carefully to avoid resistance and ensure effective treatment. For diseases like lumpy skin disease, which causes skin lesions and fever, supportive care and specific antiviral medications might be required. Always consult your veterinarian for accurate diagnosis and appropriate treatment plans.

Regularly inspect your herd for signs of disease and maintain records of any cases. This helps in tracking disease patterns and the effectiveness of treatments. Implementing proper hygiene practices, such as regular cleaning of stalls and milking equipment, can significantly reduce the risk of disease spread.

## Preventive Care And Biosecurity Practices

Preventive care and biosecurity practices are essential for safeguarding your herd from diseases and ensuring long-term productivity. Begin by implementing a comprehensive biosecurity plan that includes measures to prevent the introduction and spread of pathogens. This includes controlling access to the farm, sanitizing equipment and facilities, and ensuring that all visitors adhere to biosecurity protocols.

Isolation of new or returning animals is a key biosecurity measure. Quarantine these animals for a period to monitor for any signs of illness before integrating them into the main herd. This practice helps prevent the potential spread of diseases that could be brought in by new or previously exposed animals.

Regular cleaning and disinfection of barns, feeding areas, and water sources are crucial. Use appropriate disinfectants and follow recommended procedures to eliminate pathogens. Additionally, maintain a clean and organized environment to reduce stress on the cattle, as stress can weaken their immune systems and make them more susceptible to diseases.

# Emergency Health Management

Effective emergency health management involves being prepared for unexpected health crises and acting quickly when they occur. Start by creating an emergency health plan, which should include contact information for your veterinarian, a list of essential medications and supplies, and procedures for handling different types of emergencies, such as severe injuries or sudden illness outbreaks.

Develop a first aid kit tailored to your herd's needs, including items like bandages, antiseptics, and syringes. Train yourself and your staff in basic first aid procedures and emergency response protocols. For example, knowing how to administer first aid for wounds or perform basic life-saving measures can make a significant difference in the outcome of an emergency.

When an emergency arises, assess the situation quickly and provide initial care while awaiting professional assistance. Maintain clear records of the incident, including symptoms, treatments administered, and any changes in the animal's condition. This information will be valuable for your veterinarian in diagnosing and managing the situation effectively.

## Working With A Veterinarian And Livestock Specialists

Collaborating with a veterinarian and livestock specialists is essential for maintaining the health and productivity of your dairy herd. Start by establishing a good relationship with a qualified veterinarian who has experience with dairy cattle. They can provide valuable advice on herd management, disease prevention, and treatment strategies.

Schedule regular consultations with your veterinarian to review your herd's health status and discuss any concerns or changes in management practices. This proactive approach helps in the early detection of potential health issues and ensures that you are implementing the best practices for your herd.

In addition to your veterinarian, consider working with livestock specialists who can offer expertise in specific areas, such as nutrition, reproductive health, or genetic improvement. These specialists can provide tailored recommendations to optimize your herd's performance and address any specific challenges you may face. Regular communication and collaboration with these professionals will enhance your ability to manage your dairy herd effectively and achieve long-term success.

# CHAPTER EIGHT

## Reproduction And Breeding

## Understanding Dairy Cattle Reproduction Cycles

To effectively manage dairy cattle reproduction, it's crucial to understand their reproductive cycles. Dairy cows have a reproductive cycle known as the estrous cycle, which typically lasts about 21 days. This cycle includes four stages: proestrus, estrus, metestrus, and diestrus. During the proestrus phase, which lasts about 3-4 days, hormonal changes prepare the cow's reproductive system for ovulation. Estrus, or heat, is the period when the cow is sexually receptive and lasts about 12-18 hours. During this time, she will exhibit behavioral signs such as increased activity, restlessness, and mounting other cows.

After ovulation, the cow enters the metestrus phase, where the uterine lining begins to thicken, and the corpus luteum forms. This phase lasts about 3-5 days. Finally, in the diestrus phase, which lasts around 10-14 days, the corpus luteum maintains hormone production to support a potential pregnancy. If the cow is not pregnant, the cycle starts again with the proestrus phase. Monitoring these cycles through behavioral observations and physical examinations helps in timing insemination and optimizing breeding success.

## Breeding Methods And Selecting Breeding Stock

Choosing the right breeding method and stock is essential for improving the quality of your dairy herd. The two main breeding methods are natural mating and artificial insemination (AI). Natural mating involves allowing the bull to mate with the cows. This method is less labor-intensive but requires managing the bull's health and behavior, and the genetic improvement may be slower.

Artificial insemination is a more controlled method, where semen from a selected bull is introduced into the cow's reproductive tract. This method allows for precise genetic selection and can be more effective in improving herd quality. To use AI, collect semen from a reputable breeding center and store it in a specialized tank. Training on the correct handling and insemination technique is essential to ensure successful conception.

When selecting breeding stock, consider factors such as genetic traits, milk production, health, and conformation. Choose cows with desirable traits and bulls with proven genetics to enhance these traits in the offspring. Evaluate the herd's performance data and consult with a geneticist or breeding advisor to make informed decisions about which animals to breed.

## Managing Pregnancies And Calving

Proper management of pregnancies and calves ensures the health of both the cow and the calf. Once a cow is confirmed pregnant, monitor her closely throughout the gestation period, which lasts about 280 days. Provide a balanced diet with adequate nutrition to support the developing fetus and maintain the cow's health. Regular veterinary check-ups and vaccinations are crucial to prevent diseases that could affect the pregnancy.

As the calving date approaches, prepare a clean and comfortable birthing area for the cow. Ensure that the calving pen is well-bedded and free from drafts. When the cow begins to show signs of labor, such as restlessness or increased vaginal discharge, monitor her closely. Assist if necessary, but allow the cow to do most of the work to avoid interfering with the birthing process.

After calving, promptly check that the calf is breathing and nursing. Ensure the cow is producing adequate milk and provide her with high-quality feed and water to support lactation. Monitoring the cow and calf during this post-calving period helps in identifying any issues early and ensuring both animals remain healthy.

## Caring For Newborn Calves

The immediate care of newborn calves is critical for their survival and future health. As soon as a calf is born, ensure that it is breathing and that its airways are clear. If necessary, gently rub the calf with clean, dry towels to stimulate breathing and help it stand. Ensure that the calf begins nursing within the first few hours of life to receive colostrum, which is essential for providing immunity and energy.

Provide the calf with a clean, dry, and warm environment to prevent hypothermia. Use heat lamps or blankets if necessary to maintain a comfortable temperature. Begin feeding the calf high-quality milk replacer or colostrum and introduce solid feed, such as starter grains, as it grows. Monitor the calf's health closely, watching for signs of illness or digestive issues, and consult a veterinarian if any problems arise.

Routine vaccinations and deworming are important to protect the calf from common diseases and parasites. Implement a structured feeding and care program to ensure proper growth and development. Keeping records of each calf's growth, health status, and vaccination history helps in managing the herd effectively.

# Record-Keeping For Breeding And Reproduction

Effective record-keeping is essential for managing dairy cattle reproduction and improving herd productivity. Maintain detailed records of each cow's estrous cycle, breeding dates, and outcomes of artificial inseminations or natural matings. Document the health status, calving dates, and any interventions or treatments provided to each animal.

Use a systematic approach to record-keeping, such as digital software or a detailed spreadsheet, to track data efficiently. Include information on the genetics of breeding stock, pregnancy progress, and calving performance. Regularly review these records to identify patterns, assess the success of breeding programs, and make informed decisions about future breeding strategies.

Accurate and comprehensive records help in monitoring herd performance, managing reproductive efficiency, and making improvements to breeding practices. They also provide valuable information for veterinary consultations and future planning of herd management practices.

# CHAPTER NINE

## Dairy Farm Operations And Management

## Daily Farm Management Tasks

Dairy farm management is the backbone of a successful dairy operation. It involves a series of routine activities that ensure the smooth functioning of the farm, the well-being of the livestock, and the overall productivity of the dairy. The day begins early, often around 4 or 5 AM, with the first task being milking. Cows should be milked at consistent times every day to maintain their milk production levels and to avoid any disruptions in their routine. Milking should be done with proper hygiene practices to ensure the quality of milk and to prevent infections.

After milking, the next priority is feeding the cows. A balanced diet is essential for maintaining the health and productivity of dairy cattle. This involves providing the right mix of forage, grains, and supplements. Monitoring the cows' intake and adjusting their diet based on their production levels and health is crucial. Additionally, cleaning the feed troughs and ensuring fresh water is always available are important tasks that need to be completed.

Other daily tasks include monitoring the health of the cows, checking for any signs of illness or injury, and administering any necessary treatments. Regular inspections of the barn and equipment ensure that everything is in working order and that there are no safety hazards. Additionally, farm management tasks also involve record-keeping of milk production, feed usage, and health treatments, which helps in making informed decisions about farm operations.

# Financial Management And Record-Keeping

Financial management is a critical aspect of dairy farm operations that requires meticulous planning and execution. Keeping accurate and detailed records of all financial transactions is essential for tracking expenses and income. This includes costs related to feed, veterinary care, labor, equipment maintenance, and utilities. Using accounting software specifically designed for farm management can simplify this process, providing an overview of financial health and aiding in budgeting.

Revenue tracking involves recording sales from milk and other dairy products, as well as any additional income from by-products or services. It's important to maintain a clear distinction between personal and farm finances to ensure accurate reporting. Regularly reviewing financial statements and comparing them against budget projections helps in identifying any discrepancies or areas where costs can be reduced.

Moreover, understanding and managing cash flow is vital for sustaining operations. Farmers should be prepared for seasonal variations in income and expenses, and plan for periods of low revenue. Effective financial management also involves setting aside funds for emergency repairs or unexpected costs. Regular audits and consultations with financial advisors can provide additional support and help in making strategic decisions for long-term financial stability.

## Labor Management And Training

Effective labor management is crucial for the smooth operation of a dairy farm. This involves recruiting skilled workers, assigning clear roles and responsibilities, and ensuring that each team member is well-trained in their tasks.

Proper training includes teaching employees about animal care, milking procedures, equipment operation, and safety protocols. Regular training sessions and updates on best practices help maintain high standards of farm management.

Creating a positive work environment is also important for retaining employees. This can be achieved through fair compensation, opportunities for advancement, and recognition of good performance. Open communication between management and workers helps in addressing any concerns promptly and fosters a cooperative atmosphere.

Additionally, labor management includes scheduling shifts to ensure that the farm operates smoothly around the clock. This involves planning for peak milking times, feedings, and maintenance tasks while considering employee work hours and rest periods.

Efficient scheduling minimizes downtime and maximizes productivity, contributing to the overall success of the dairy operation.

## Marketing And Selling Dairy Products

Marketing and selling dairy products effectively requires a well-thought-out strategy to reach potential customers and build a strong market presence. Start by identifying your target market, which could include local grocery stores, restaurants, or direct-to-consumer sales through farmer's markets and online platforms. Understanding consumer preferences and trends can guide product offerings and pricing strategies.

Developing a strong brand identity helps in differentiating your products from competitors. This includes creating appealing packaging, establishing a memorable brand name, and promoting your dairy products through various channels such as social media, local advertising, and community events. Offering product samples or conducting taste tests can attract new customers and generate positive word-of-mouth.

Additionally, building relationships with distributors and retailers can help in expanding your market reach. Networking within the industry and participating in trade shows or agricultural fairs can provide valuable exposure and open up new sales opportunities. Effective marketing not only drives sales but also builds customer loyalty and enhances the overall reputation of your dairy farm.

## Implementing Sustainable Farming Practices

Implementing sustainable farming practices is essential for the long-term success and environmental stewardship of a dairy operation.

Start by assessing the farm's current practices and identifying areas where improvements can be made. This could involve reducing waste, conserving water, and optimizing energy use. For instance, using energy-efficient equipment and recycling waste products can lower operational costs and minimize environmental impact.

Sustainable farming also involves improving soil health and promoting biodiversity. Practices such as crop rotation, using organic fertilizers, and maintaining natural habitats can enhance soil fertility and support a balanced ecosystem. Additionally, integrating manure management systems that recycle waste into compost or biogas can further contribute to sustainability.

Engaging in community and industry initiatives focused on sustainability can provide additional resources and support. This includes participating in certification programs or sustainability audits that validate the farm's efforts and offer guidance on best practices. By adopting sustainable practices, dairy farmers not only contribute to environmental conservation but also improve the overall efficiency and resilience of their farm operations.

# CHAPTER TEN

## Troubleshooting Common Issues

## Identifying And Solving Common Dairy Farming Problems

Dairy farming can present a variety of challenges, and recognizing common problems early can help prevent them from escalating. A frequent issue is mastitis, an infection of the udder, which can reduce milk yield and affect milk quality. To identify mastitis, look for signs such as swelling, redness, or heat in the udder, as well as abnormal milk consistency. Regularly monitor your cows' udder health by performing physical exams and using a mastitis test, which detects abnormal milk composition.

Another common problem is lameness in dairy cows, often caused by poor hoof care or infections. Cows may exhibit signs of lameness by limping, standing on three legs, or avoiding walking. To address this, ensure regular hoof trimming every 6-8 weeks and inspect hooves for any injuries or signs of infection. Providing a clean and comfortable resting area for cows also helps prevent hoof problems. In case of serious infections, consult a veterinarian for appropriate treatment.

Nutritional deficiencies can also impact dairy production. If cows are not producing enough milk or showing signs of poor health, check their diet to ensure it meets their nutritional requirements. A balanced diet should include adequate levels of protein, fiber, and minerals. Work with a nutritionist to formulate a feed plan that supports optimal milk production and overall health.

## Addressing Equipment Failures And Repairs

Maintaining equipment in good working condition is crucial for efficient dairy farming. Milking machines, feeders, and cooling systems are central to daily operations and must be regularly inspected and serviced. Start by creating a maintenance schedule for all your equipment. For milking machines, this includes daily cleaning and monthly checks of vacuum levels and teat cup liners to prevent malfunctions.

In case of equipment failure, such as a malfunctioning milking machine, follow these steps: first, identify the problem by checking for obvious signs like unusual noises or incomplete milking. Next, consult the equipment's manual for troubleshooting tips or error codes. For issues beyond basic fixes, contact a professional technician who specializes in dairy equipment repair. Keeping spare parts on hand for common issues can minimize downtime and ensure smooth operations.

Feeder systems may also face issues such as blockages or mechanical failures. Regularly inspect and clean feeders to prevent feed clogs and ensure that they are dispensing the correct amounts. If you encounter a problem, stop the feeder, clear any obstructions, and check for worn-out parts. Routine maintenance can prevent many common failures and extend the lifespan of your equipment.

## Handling Unexpected Health And Production Issues

Unexpected health issues can disrupt dairy production and impact overall farm performance. To manage these issues, establish a health monitoring system for your herd. This involves regularly checking cows for signs of illness and maintaining accurate health records. If a cow shows signs of illness, such as decreased milk production or changes in behavior, isolate her from the rest of the herd to prevent disease spread and consult with a veterinarian for a proper diagnosis and treatment plan.

Production issues may include a sudden drop in milk yield or changes in milk quality. Investigate potential causes such as changes in diet, health problems, or environmental conditions. Adjust the cows' diet or improve their living conditions as needed. Keeping detailed records of production metrics and any changes in management practices will help you identify patterns and potential solutions.

In case of an outbreak of disease, such as bovine tuberculosis or foot-and-mouth disease, follow biosecurity measures to contain the spread. This includes quarantining affected animals, disinfecting equipment and facilities, and notifying local agricultural authorities. Prompt action and adherence to biosecurity protocols are essential for managing disease outbreaks effectively.

# Dealing With Market Fluctuations

Market fluctuations can affect dairy farming profitability, with prices for milk varying due to supply and demand changes, trade policies, or global market trends. To mitigate the impact of market fluctuations, consider diversifying your farm's income sources. For example, you might explore value-added products such as cheese or yogurt, which can offer higher margins and reduce dependence on fluctuating milk prices.

Implementing a financial management plan that includes budgeting and forecasting can help you navigate periods of low milk prices. Monitor market trends and adjust your production levels accordingly to avoid oversupply.

Additionally, establishing contracts or joining a dairy cooperative can provide more stable pricing and reduce the risk associated with market volatility.

Stay informed about market conditions by subscribing to industry reports and participating in local dairy farming organizations. Networking with other dairy farmers can provide insights into market trends and offer support during challenging times. Adapting your business strategy based on market information will help you manage fluctuations and maintain financial stability.

## Seeking Support And Resources For Problem-Solving

Accessing support and resources is essential for effectively addressing dairy farming issues. Start by joining industry associations or local dairy farming groups where you can exchange knowledge and experiences with other farmers.

These networks often provide valuable resources such as training programs, expert advice, and industry updates.

Leverage online resources and platforms that offer guidance on dairy farming practices. Many agricultural extension services and university programs provide free or low-cost resources, including troubleshooting guides, webinars, and technical support. Utilize these resources to stay informed about best practices and solutions for common problems.

Consider consulting with agricultural consultants or veterinarians who specialize in dairy farming. These professionals can offer tailored advice based on your specific farm conditions and help you implement effective solutions. Building relationships with trusted advisors will provide ongoing support and expertise to address any challenges that arise.

By understanding and addressing common dairy farming issues with practical strategies, maintaining equipment, managing health and production concerns, navigating market fluctuations, and seeking appropriate support, you can ensure a smoother and more successful dairy farming operation.

# Frequently Asked A Question And Their Answers

**What is dairy farming?**

Dairy farming is the practice of raising cattle for milk production, which is then processed into various dairy products such as milk, cheese, butter, and yogurt.

**What breeds of cows are commonly used in dairy farming?**

Common dairy cow breeds include Holstein, Jersey, Guernsey, Ayrshire, and Brown Swiss. Holsteins are the most widely used due to their high milk production.

**How much milk does a dairy cow produce daily?**

On average, a dairy cow can produce between 6 to 7 gallons (22 to 26 liters) of milk per day.

### What do dairy cows eat?

Dairy cows typically eat a balanced diet of hay, silage (fermented grass or corn), grains, and supplements to ensure they receive all necessary nutrients.

### How often are dairy cows milked?

Dairy cows are usually milked two to three times a day to maintain milk production and cow health.

### What is the lifespan of a dairy cow?

The average lifespan of a dairy cow is about 5 to 6 years in commercial dairy operations, although they can live longer with proper care.

### How are dairy cows cared for?

Dairy cows require regular veterinary care, a balanced diet, clean water, comfortable housing, and proper milking procedures to maintain their health and productivity.

## What is pasteurization, and why is it important?

Pasteurization is the process of heating milk to a specific temperature for a set period to kill harmful bacteria. It is important to ensure the safety and extend the shelf life of milk and dairy products.

## What are the environmental impacts of dairy farming?

Dairy farming can have environmental impacts, including greenhouse gas emissions, water usage, and land use. Sustainable practices and technologies are being developed to mitigate these effects.

## How do farmers ensure the quality of milk?

Farmers ensure milk quality through proper cow nutrition, hygiene, regular health checks, and maintaining clean milking equipment and facilities.

## What are the main challenges in dairy farming?

Challenges include fluctuating milk prices, disease management, labor shortages, and environmental regulations.

## What is organic dairy farming?

Organic dairy farming involves raising cows without synthetic fertilizers, pesticides, or genetically modified organisms (GMOs), and adhering to strict organic certification standards.

## How is milk transported from the farm to the processing plant?

Milk is transported in refrigerated tanker trucks from the farm to the processing plant to maintain its freshness and quality.

**What are some common dairy products made from milk?**

Common dairy products include milk, cheese, butter, yogurt, ice cream, and cream.

**How does the milking process work?**

The milking process involves cleaning the cow's udder, attaching milking machines to the teats, and collecting the milk in sanitized containers or pipelines.

**What role do veterinarians play in dairy farming?**

Veterinarians help maintain cow health through regular check-ups, disease prevention, and treatment of illnesses.

**How is dairy farming different from beef farming?**

Dairy farming focuses on milk production from cows, while beef farming raises cattle primarily for meat. The breeds, management practices, and diets differ between the two.

**What is the significance of artificial insemination in dairy farming?**

Artificial insemination allows for selective breeding, improving milk production, cow health, and genetics in the herd.

**How do dairy farmers manage manure and waste?**

Manure management involves proper storage, composting, and spreading on fields as fertilizer, along with using technologies to reduce odors and environmental impact.

**What advancements are being made in dairy farming technology?**

Advancements include robotic milking systems, automated feeding systems, precision farming tools, genetic improvements, and sustainable farming practices to enhance efficiency and productivity.

# CONCLUSION

Dairy farming stands at a critical crossroads, with evolving challenges and opportunities shaping its future. This sector, integral to the global food supply, faces significant pressures from economic, environmental, and social fronts. As we look to the future, the sustainability and efficiency of dairy farming must be paramount to meet the growing demands of a burgeoning global population while mitigating environmental impacts.

One of the primary challenges facing dairy farming is the need for environmental sustainability. The dairy industry is a significant source of greenhouse gas emissions, primarily methane, which contributes to climate change. To address this, farmers are increasingly adopting practices such as improved manure management, feed efficiency, and pasture management.

Technological advancements, including methane digesters and precision farming tools, offer promising solutions to reduce the carbon footprint of dairy operations. Embracing these innovations is crucial for the industry to align with global climate goals and regulatory requirements.

Economic viability remains a critical concern for dairy farmers, who must navigate volatile milk prices, rising production costs, and competition from plant-based alternatives. Diversification and value-added products, such as artisanal cheeses and organic milk, can provide farmers with new revenue streams and greater financial resilience. Additionally, direct-to-consumer models and local marketing initiatives enable farmers to capture a larger share of the retail dollar, fostering stronger connections with consumers and communities.

Animal welfare is another key focus area, with increasing public scrutiny on farming practices. High standards of animal care are essential not only for ethical reasons but also for ensuring high-quality milk production. Practices such as providing comfortable living conditions, proper nutrition, and regular health check-ups are fundamental. Certification programs and transparent reporting can help build consumer trust and support for dairy products.

The social dimension of dairy farming is also evolving, with a growing recognition of the role of family farms and rural communities. Supporting the next generation of dairy farmers is vital to the industry's sustainability. Programs that provide education, training, and financial support can empower young farmers to adopt modern practices and technologies. Furthermore, promoting gender equality and inclusivity within the sector can unlock new perspectives and innovations, driving the industry forward.

In conclusion, the future of dairy farming hinges on a balanced approach that integrates environmental stewardship, economic resilience, animal welfare, and social responsibility. By embracing innovation, sustainability, and community engagement, the dairy industry can navigate its current challenges and continue to play a vital role in global food security. The path forward requires collaboration among farmers, policymakers, researchers, and consumers to create a resilient and sustainable dairy farming sector that benefits all stakeholders. As we advance, a commitment to continuous improvement and adaptation will be essential to ensuring the long-term viability and success of dairy farming.

# THE END

www.ingramcontent.com/pod-product-compliance
Lightning Source LLC
Chambersburg PA
CBHW071833210526
45479CB00001B/119